The Story of Jonah

SIMON & SCHUSTER
LONDON • SYDNEY • NEW YORK • TOKYO • SINGAPORE • TORONTO

Why is Jonah trying to escape on a boat?
What would you like to escape from?

What is it like for the people on the boat during the storm?

Why do you think the captain has told his crew to throw Jonah into the sea?

What would you do if you were the captain?

How do you think Jonah is feeling?

What frightening things have ever happened to you?

Who is Jonah talking to?

Who helps you when you are in trouble?

Why is the fish being sick?

How do you think Jonah is feeling as he walks into Nineveh?

What do you ever have to do that you don't want to?

Why are the people sorry for the things they have done?

What kinds of things are you sorry you have said or done?

Why is Jonah feeling cross?

When do you feel cross?

What makes Jonah feel better?

Why has God sent the worm to eat the plant?
What would you have done if you were God?